SELF-CONTROL

by

Carole MacKenthun, R.S.M.
and Paulinus Dwyer, O.P.

illustrated by Vanessa Filkins

Cover by Vanessa Filkins

Songs by Kathy Jones, Frances Mann Benson and Helen Kitchell Evans

ISBN No. 0-86653-396-6

Standardized Subject Code TA ac

Printing No. 98

Shining Star Publications
A Division of Good Apple, Inc.
Box 299
Carthage, IL 62321-0299

Unless otherwise indicated, the King James version of the Bible was used in preparing the activities in this book.

DEDICATION

For the St. Matthias School community in Somerset, New Jersey.

INTRODUCTION

''And every man that striveth for the mastery is temperate in all things . . . .''
I Corinthians 9:25

There are cravings within us that make us wish to do things that work against the harmony that should exist between others and ourselves. Our bodies always want to go to extremes. Self-control is using God's good things in balance.

The Holy Spirit gives us the inner strength to control these urges within us. In order to grow in the virtue of self-control we must practice over and over. In Corinthians, Paul tells us that we must strive as an athlete does. We must do difficult things again and again to develop a habit that will become a part of us.

The purpose of this book is to assist parents and religious educators in teaching about this needed gift of self-control. Contained in this book are work sheets, games, songs, puzzles and a prayer service that will motivate children to learn what the Bible teaches about this virtue and how we can practice it. A scriptural passage on self-control is listed at the top of most pages, and more references are given in the back of the book for reflection or for follow-up activities.

TABLE OF CONTENTS

SELF-CONTROL AND TELEVISION

"Watch and pray, that ye enter not into temptation . . . ." Matthew 26:41

A. As you watch your favorite TV program, look for situations in which self-control enters into the plot.

B. Find one example of self-control from each of the following types of shows and write a brief summary of the situation.

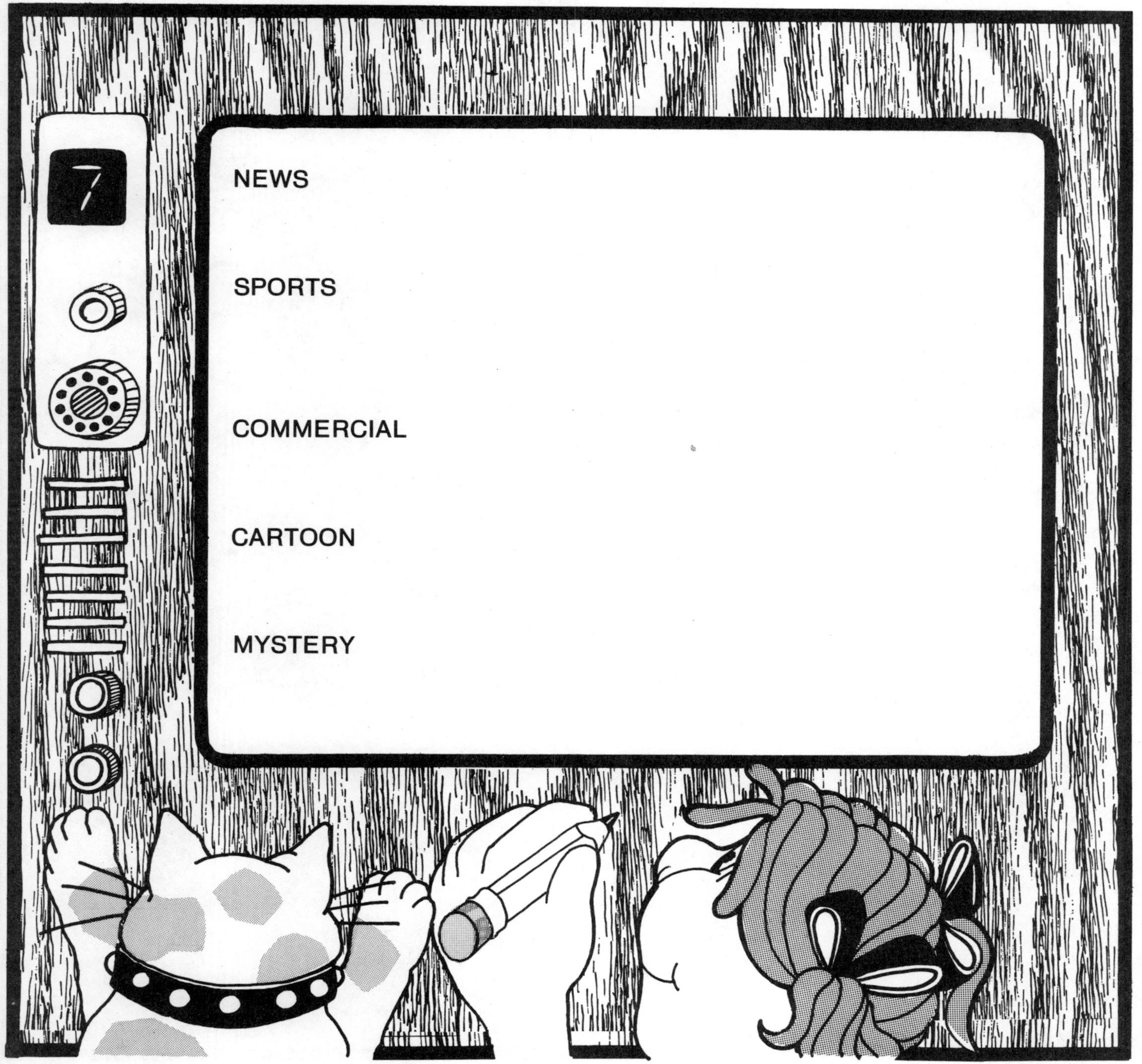

KEYS TO SELF-CONTROL

"... temperance: against such there is no law." Galatians 5:23

Listed below are some possible ways to acquire self-control. Write some of your own suggestions in the empty keys. Cut out your most important key to self-control and put a piece of yarn through it. Hang it on your bedroom door and remember to read it each day.

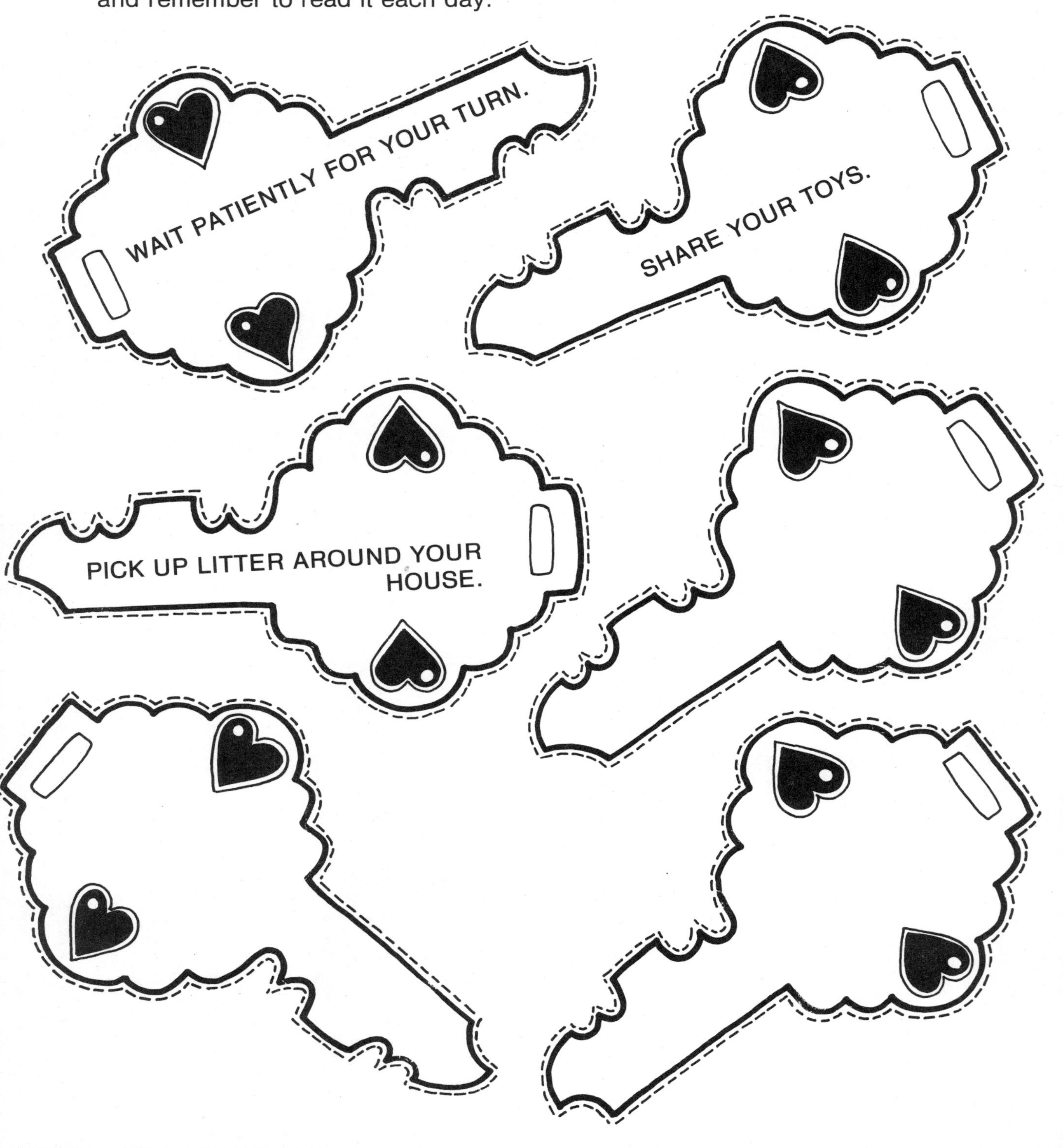

FOLLOWING JESUS

"Be ye therefore followers of God, as dear children; And walk in love, as Christ also hath loved us, and hath given himself for us . . . ." Ephesians 5:1,2

Locate the places where the following incidents occurred, as shown on the map on the next page. Write the grid number and letter next to the incident which took place there and name the location in the blank provided. Read Matthew 26-27, Mark 14-15, Luke 22-23, and John 18-19 to find the answers.

1. Garden where Jesus prayed 3 H Gethsemane
2. Home of the Roman governor __ __ ____________
3. Where Jesus died __ __ ____________
4. Where Jesus ate with His Apostles __ __ ____________
5. Judas betrayed Jesus __ __ ____________
6. Soldiers gambled for Jesus' clothes __ __ ____________
7. Jesus questioned at Caiphas' house __ __ ____________
8. Place of Resurrection __ __ ____________
9. Disciples all ran away __ __ ____________
10. Soldiers put crown of thorns on Jesus' head __ __ ____________
11. Peter's denial __ __ ____________
12. Jesus buried __ __ ____________
13. Jesus nailed to the cross __ __ ____________
14. Jesus condemned to death __ __ ____________
15. Jesus taken to Pilate __ __ ____________
16. Soldiers arrested Jesus __ __ ____________
17. Jesus' friends slept __ __ ____________
18. Jesus taken to Herod __ __ ____________
19. Soldiers scourged Jesus __ __ ____________
20. Crossed Cedron Brook __ __ ____________

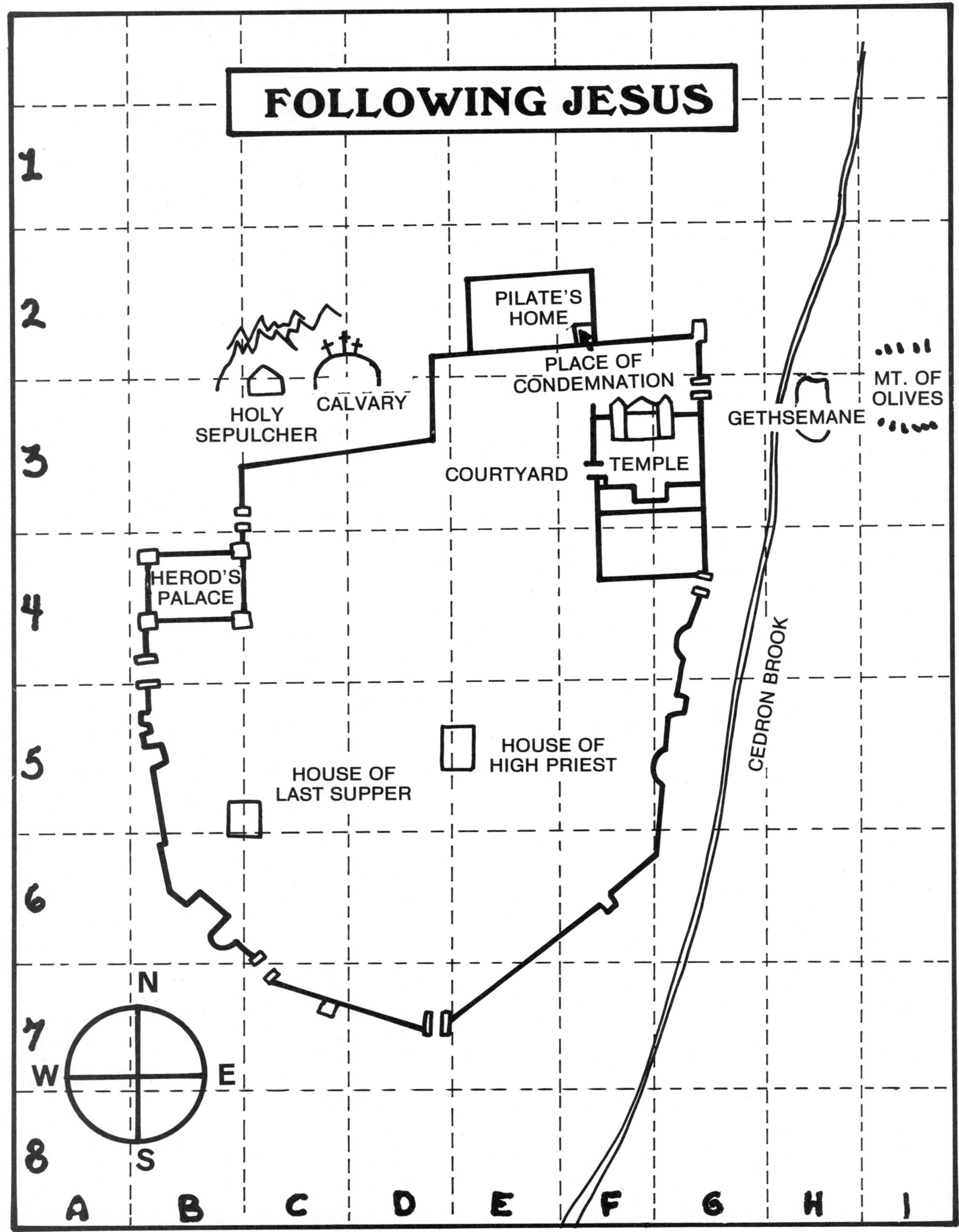
FOLLOWING JESUS
PILATE'S HOME
PLACE OF CONDEMNATION
MT. OF OLIVES
HOLY SEPULCHER
CALVARY
GETHSEMANE
TEMPLE
COURTYARD
HEROD'S PALACE
CEDRON BROOK
HOUSE OF HIGH PRIEST
HOUSE OF LAST SUPPER
N
W
E
S
1
2
3
4
5
6
7
8
A
B
C
D
E
F
G
H
I

JEZEBEL AND KING AHAB

"The mighty man, and the man of war, the judge, and the prophet, and the prudent, and the ancient . . . ."
Isaiah 3:2

Read the story of King Ahab and his wife Jezebel. Greed led them to commit a terrible crime.

Read I Kings 21:1-16; 22:31-40; and II Kings 9:30-37; then follow the story through the maze. Think how you could want something so much that you might do wrong to get it. How would you show self-control in this circumstance?

Write about this temptation and tell how you would cope with it.

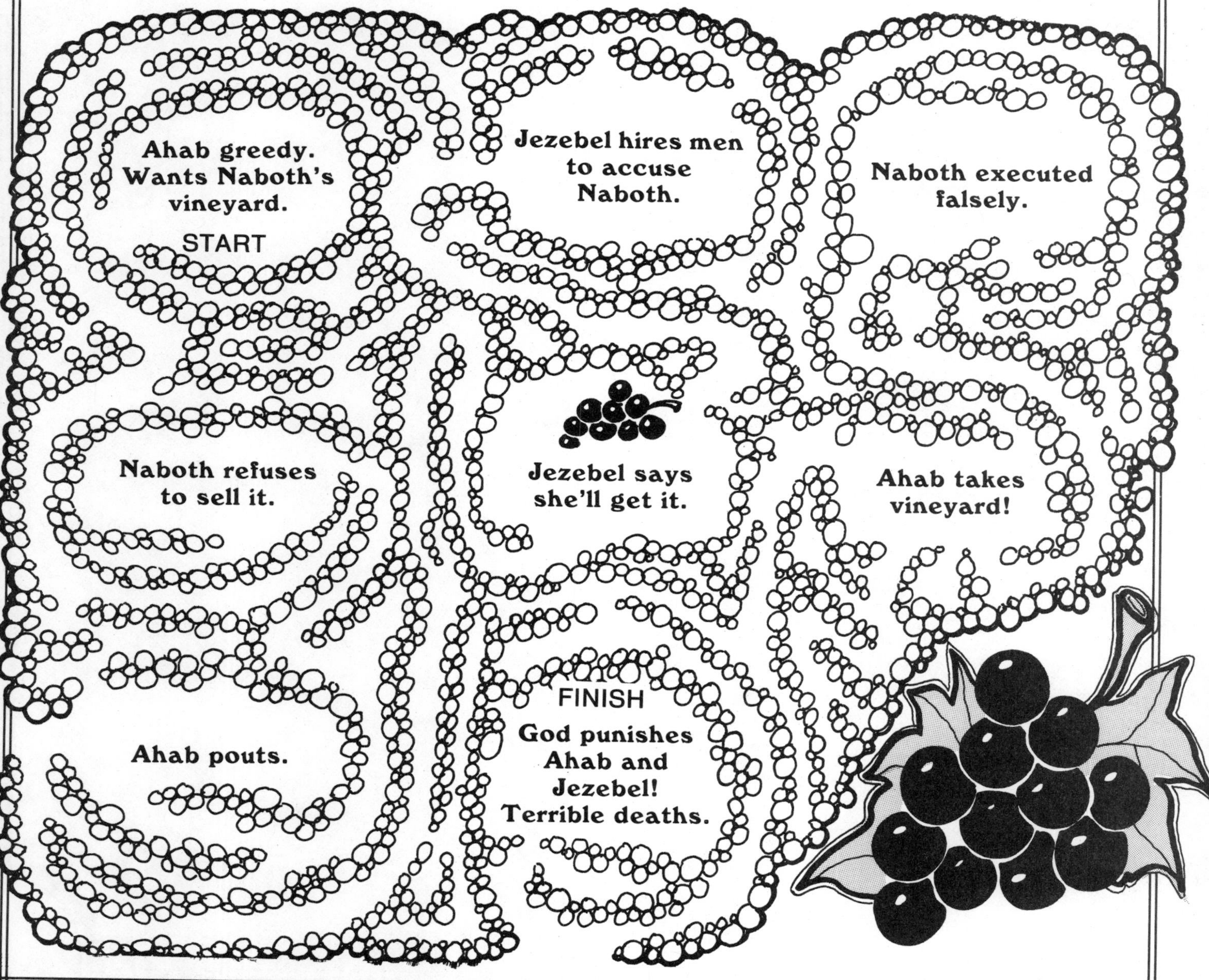

HEROES

"But a lover of hospitality, a lover of good men, sober, just, holy, temperate."
Titus 1:8

There are heroes in our lives whom we look to as models when we are faced with great difficulties. A hero or heroine is someone we admire for bravery, great deeds and noble qualities. Is there someone who is a model for you when you have to make a decision not to do something wrong? How does this person exemplify self-control? In the space below tell about this person. Explain who he is, and why he is your hero. What has he done to merit your admiration? When might you try to imitate him?

FIVE LOAVES AND TWO FISHES

''And they did eat, and were all filled: and there was taken up of fragments that remained to them twelve baskets.'' Luke 9:17

Jesus taught us about self-control in the story of the multiplication of the loaves and fishes Luke 9:11-17. (an adaptation)

> Taking the five loaves and the two fishes, Jesus pronounced a blessing over them, broke them, and gave them to His Disciples for distribution to the crowd. They all ate until they had enough. What they had left, over and above, filled twelve baskets.

Notice that the people did not overeat or take the leftovers. They ate what they needed and allowed the extra to be collected by the Disciples.

Pretend that you are writing a sequel to this story. What do you think the Disciples did with the twelve baskets that remained? Write your ideas in the space provided.

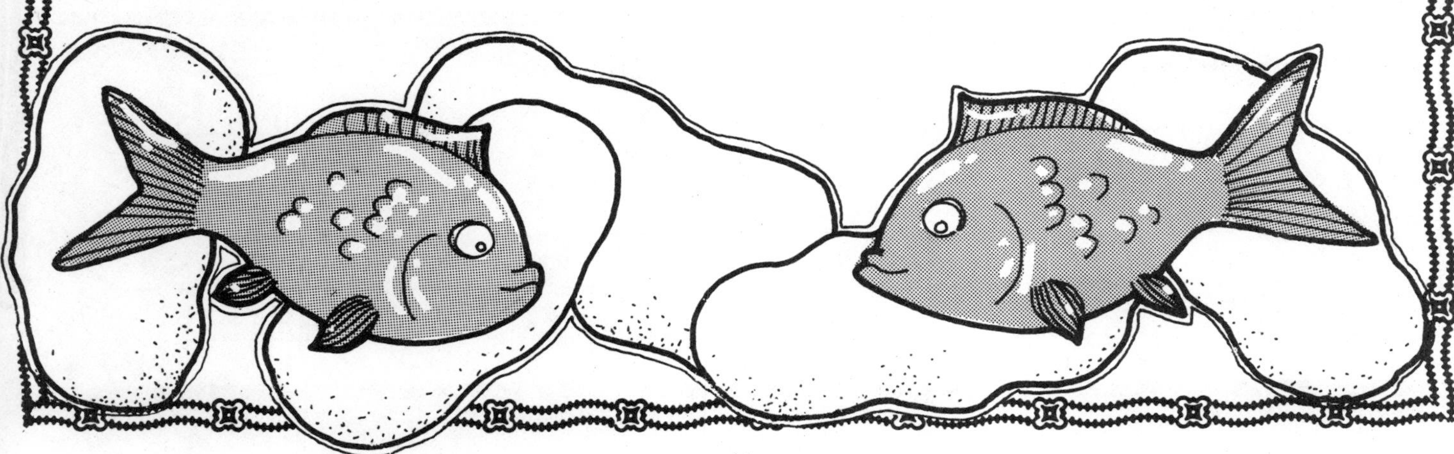

JESUS IN THE TEMPLE

"And as he reasoned of righteousness, temperance, and judgment to come . . . ."
Acts 24:25

Greed is wanting to take more than one's fair share. Frequently this means that one acts with dishonesty in trying to gain it. Because we constantly have an urge to increase what seems good to us, self-control is always needed to keep our desires in check.

Read the story of Jesus in the temple in John 2:13-25, Matthew 21:12-16, Mark 11:15-19, and Luke 19:45-48.

Pretend that you are a TV reporter sent to cover the Passover feast during Jesus' time. Interview each of the following people and give their reactions in two or three sentences. Show what attitude each might have toward greed or self-control.

A MONEY CHANGER

____
____
____
____
____
____

A BYSTANDER

____
____
____
____
____
____

AN ANIMAL SELLER

____
____
____
____
____

A DOVE SELLER

____
____
____
____
____

A CHIEF PRIEST

____
____
____
____
____

JESUS

____
____
____
____
____

SEVEN YEARS OF FAMINE

Joseph showed self-control many times in his life. Study the story of Joseph, found in Genesis 37-50. Make a list of seven times that Joseph had to show great courage and self-control. Then play the game found on this page.

To play this game you will need a bag of dried corn, a marker for each player and one die. The object of the game is to get through the seven years of famine without running out of food. This game can be played by 1-4 players.

1. Give each player ten pieces of corn.
2. Place each player's marker in the first space.
3. Take turns rolling the die and moving the number of spaces indicated on the die.
4. If you land on a question and can correctly answer it, you get five more pieces of corn. If you land on a question and cannot answer it, you lose three pieces of corn.
5. If you run out of corn during the game, you lose. If you make it to the end of the board, you win! If several people are playing and make it to the end of the board, the player with the most pieces of corn is declared the winner.

START

1 What present did Joseph's father give him?

2 What was Joseph's dream that made his brothers so angry?

3 Why did Joseph's father send him to the fields to find his brothers?

4 Whom did Joseph's brothers sell for twenty pieces of silver?

5 What did Joseph say the butler's dream meant?

6 What did Joseph say the baker's dream meant?

7 What dream did Pharaoh have?

8 What did Joseph say Pharaoh's dream meant?

9 Of what did Pharaoh put Joseph in charge?

10 Why did Joseph travel to Egypt for Pharaoh?

11 How did Joseph save many lives in Egypt and Israel?

12 Why did Joseph's brothers come to Egypt?

13 Whom did Joseph send his brothers back to Israel to get?

14 What did Joseph tell his brothers after he sent the Egyptians out of the room?

15 When Joseph forgave his brothers, what did he tell them?

FINISH

PAUL'S MESSAGE

Self-control is a virtue which helps us to accept difficulties. We often must do without something which we very much want, in order to have something which is better for us. A dieter may sometimes do without dessert to help his heart grow stronger. In the same way, Paul tells his friends in Rome that suffering helps to build stronger character.

Decode the message of Paul below.

CODE:

A oo	E o	I ool	M ⊙·	Q ÷o	U ≗	Y ·⊙
B ɸ	F ll	J loo	N l	R ō	V ō̿	Z ⊙
C ol	G olo	K ooo	O llo	S o̲	W %	
D lo	H lol	L lll	P oll	T ⊕	X ɸ̸	

% o   o ɸ̸ ≗ lll ⊕   ool l   o̲ ≗ ll ll o ō ool l olo o̲

oo lll o̲ llo   ooo l llo % ool l olo   ⊕ lol oo ⊕   o̲ ≗ ll ll o ō ool l olo

% llo ō ooo o̲   o l lo ≗ ō oo l ol o   oo l lo   o l lo ≗ ō oo l ol o

oll ō llo lo ≗ ol o o̲   ō̿ ool ō ⊕ ≗ o,   oo l lo   ō̿ ool ō ⊕ ≗ o

lol llo oll o.   oo l lo   lol llo oll o   lo llo o o̲   l llo ⊕

lo ool o̲ oo oll oll llo ool l ⊕,   ɸ o ol oo ≗ o̲ o   ⊕ lol o   lll llo ō̿ o

llo ll   olo llo lo   ool o̲   oll llo ≗ ō o lo   ll llo ō ⊕ lol   ool l

llo ≗ ō   lol o oo ō ⊕ o̲   ɸ ·⊙   ⊕ lol o   lol llo lll ·⊙

o̲ oll ool ō ool ⊕   % lol llo   lol oo o̲   ɸ o o l   olo ool ō̿ o l

⊕ llo   ≗ o̲.

BONUS:
Read again the advice that Paul gives to his friends and Christian converts in Rome, in Romans 5:3-5. Write a letter to Paul telling how you would respond to his advice.

SOURCES OF STRENGTH

''Woe unto them that are wise in their own eyes, and prudent in their own sight!''

Isaiah 5:21

On the day of Pentecost, the Apostles were filled with the Holy Spirit. (Acts 10:44-48.) All of Jesus' followers are also given this Spirit. (Romans 5:5.) God has poured His love into our hearts and lives to strengthen us. The Spirit helps each of us according to our needs. (I Corinthians 12:7-11.)

In this maze are found words characterizing strength. See if you can find them. Letters may go up, down, forward, backward or even twist. The same letter may be used more than once. Keep a list of the words you find.

FIND THESE WORDS IN THE MAZE:
adore; courage; fear; holy; honor; integrity; judgment; knowledge; pain; peace; pray; respect; revere; reverence; sacrifice; understanding; virtue; wisdom

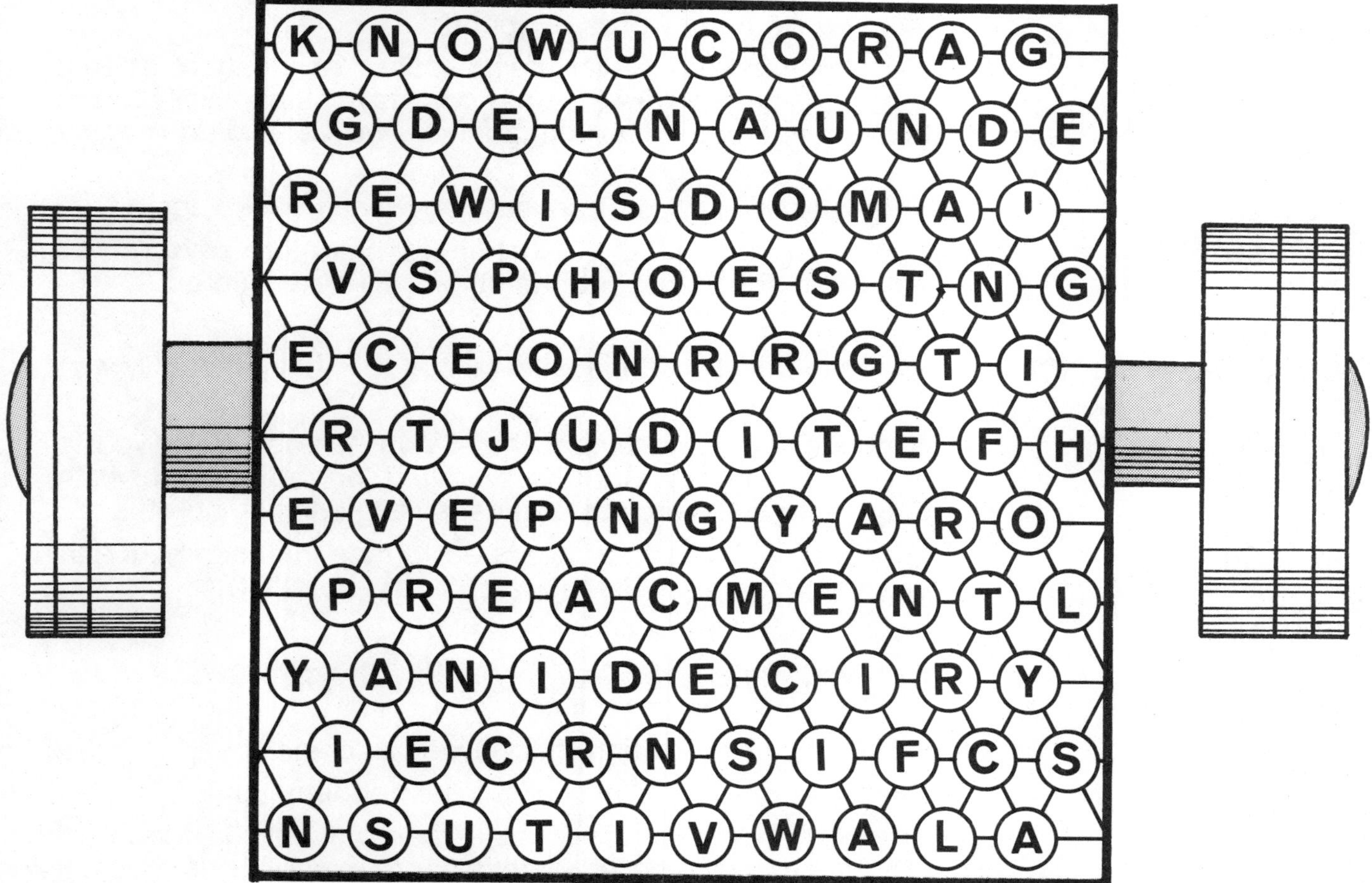

BONUS:
Choose one word from the maze and tell how its application might improve your life.

PETER LEARNS THE HARD WAY

"The simple believeth every word: but the prudent man looketh well to his going."

Proverbs 14:15

Sometimes when we do something wrong we are sorry. We don't want to do it again, and so we try hard to avoid the same action in the future. As a result we become better because of our mistake.

In this play you will see that this is what happened to Simon Peter. After his denial of Jesus, he became a great Christian and was able to lead many others to love Jesus as he did.

You may want to act this play out with your friends, or you may use the finger puppet patterns on page 18.

NARRATOR: As it grew dark, Jesus arrived with the Twelve. They reclined at the table, and during the course of the meal Jesus spoke:

JESUS: I have greatly desired to eat this Passover with you before I suffer.

NARRATOR: While they were eating, a dispute arose among the Twelve. Jesus gave them words of counsel.

JESUS: Earthly kings lord it over their people. Yet it cannot be that way with you. You are the ones who have stood loyally by me in my temptation. In my kingdom you will eat and drink at my table.

NARRATOR: They all sang songs of praise; then Jesus spoke again.

JESUS: Your faith in me shall be shaken, for Scripture says, "I will strike the shepherd, and the sheep will be scattered."

NARRATOR: Peter spoke.

PETER: Even though all are shaken in faith, it will not be that way with me.

JESUS: Simon, Simon! Remember that Satan has asked for you to sift you like wheat. But I have prayed for you that your faith may never fail. You in turn must strengthen your brothers.

PETER: Lord, at your side I am prepared to face imprisonment and death itself.

NARRATOR: Jesus gave Peter a startling reply.

JESUS: I tell you, Peter, this very day before the cock crows twice, you will deny me three times.

NARRATOR: But Peter kept insisting that he would remain loyal.

PETER: Even if I have to die with you, I will not deny you!

NARRATOR: Then they went out and made their way to the Mount of Olives, to a place called Gethsemane. It was Jesus' custom to come here to pray.

JESUS: Stay here and pray that you may not be put to the test.

NARRATOR: He withdrew about a stone's throw and knelt to pray. Then an angel appeared to Him from heaven to strengthen Him. When He arose from prayer, He came to His Disciples, only to find them asleep.

JESUS:	Why are you sleeping? Wake up, and pray that you may not enter into temptation.
NARRATOR:	He went to pray a second time. And He came a second time and found them sleeping again. He said to Peter:
JESUS:	Asleep, Simon? Could you not stay awake for even one hour? Be on your guard that you be not tempted! The spirit is indeed willing, but nature is weak.''
NARRATOR:	While He was still speaking, a crowd came. When the companions of Jesus saw what was going to happen, they wondered what to do.
ALL:	Lord, shall we use the sword?
NARRATOR:	Then Peter went so far as to strike the high priest's servant and cut off his right ear. But Jesus rebuked him.
JESUS:	Put up your sword into its scabbard. Bear with them thus far.
NARRATOR:	Then He touched Malchus' ear and healed it. Jesus was then led away, placed under arrest and brought to the house of the high priest. Peter followed at a distance. Later a fire was lighted in the middle of the courtyard, and Peter sat beside it, along with some other people. A servant girl saw him sitting in the light of the fire. She looked at him intently, then said:
GIRL:	This man was with Him.
NARRATOR:	Peter denied the fact.
PETER:	Woman, I do not know Him.
NARRATOR:	Peter then went out to the gateway. There another maid saw him and said:
MAID:	This man also was with Jesus of Nazareth.
NARRATOR:	But Peter denied it with an oath:
PETER:	I do not know the man.
NARRATOR:	And a cock crowed. About an hour later, a bystander came up and said to Peter:
MAN:	Surely you are also one of them. You even talk like a Galilean.
NARRATOR:	Peter began to curse and to swear.
PETER:	I do not even know the man you are talking about.
NARRATOR:	Just then a second cock's crow was heard. At that very moment Jesus turned around and looked at Peter. Peter remembered the warning that Jesus had made: ''Before the cock crows two times, you will deny me three times.'' Peter broke down and began to weep. And he went out crying bitterly.

BONUS:
You may wish to read this story of Peter's denial in Matthew 26:30-46, 51-54, 69-75 and Mark 14:26; 47:66-72; and Luke 22:29-34; 39-46; 49-51; 54-62; John 13:36-38; 18:10-18; 25-27.

PUPPET PATTERNS FOR PETER LEARNS THE HARD WAY

Color each puppet and cut out. Adjust the tabs so they fit snugly around your fingers, or cut off the tabs and attach a Popsicle stick to the bottom of each puppet.

PRACTICING SELF-CONTROL
A CLASS COVENANT

A covenant is an agreement between two people or two groups of people. God made several covenants with the people of the Old Testament. The word covenant first appears in the Bible in the story of Noah. After the flood, God made a covenant with all living things. He promised that He would never again destroy the world by flood.

In a covenant, those who are making the agreement list the things they agree to do. Then both sides sign the agreement and promise to keep the covenant. Write your own covenant. Choose something that you need to work on. You may want to get input from the person or group of people with whom you are making your covenant. When you finish writing your covenant, sign it and have it signed by the other appropriate person or persons.

CIRCLE OF TIME

"To every thing there is a season, and a time to every purpose under heaven."
Ecclesiastes 3:1

Each section of the circle represents one hour of the day. Mark off the circle in sections, showing the amount of time you spend doing various activities throughout the day. Label these activities.

Next look at your circle of time. Are you giving some time to God? To others? Are you spending too much time on yourself?

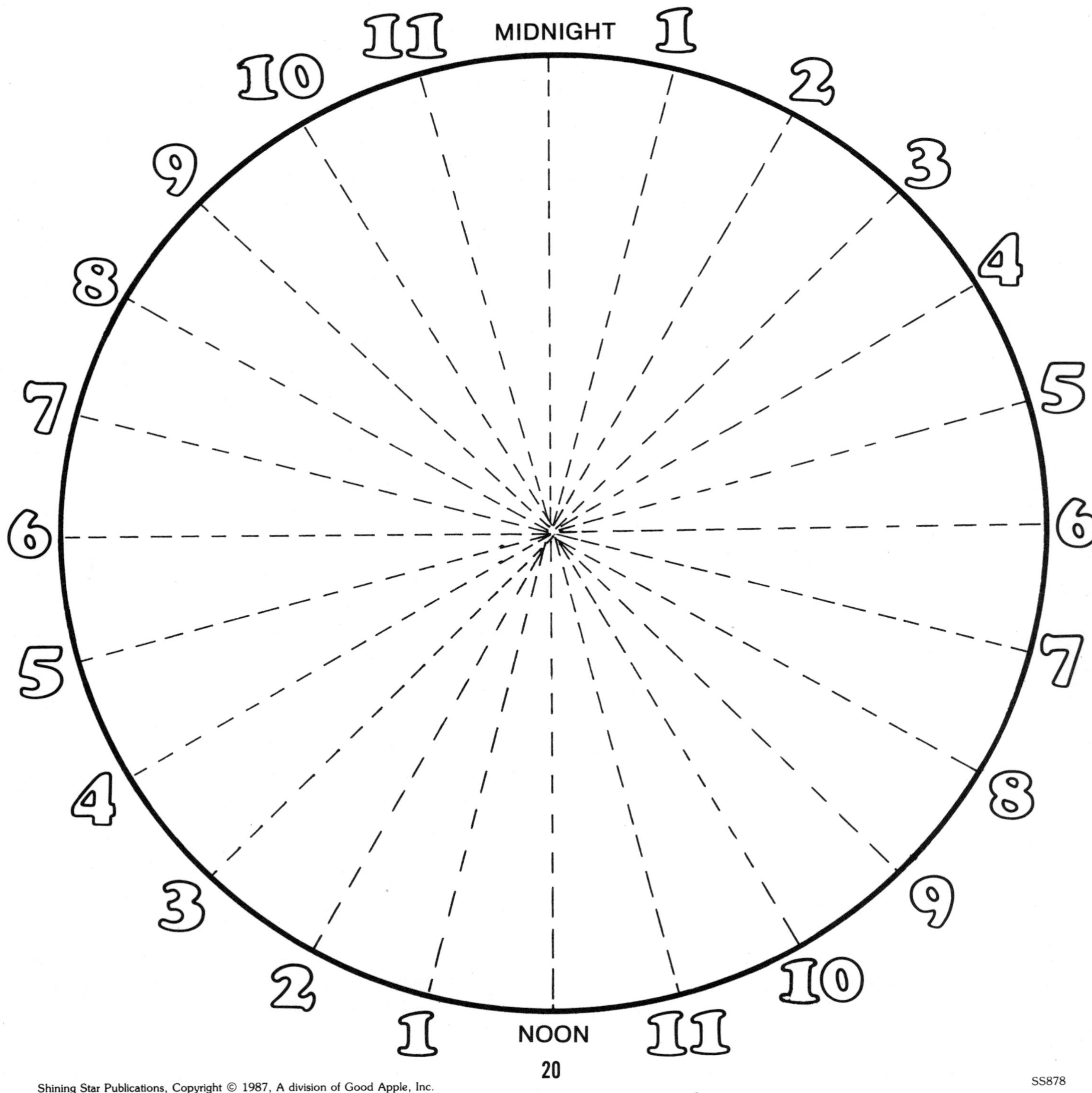

PERSONAL REDUCTION PLAN

''A fool's wrath is presently known: but a prudent man covereth shame.''
Proverbs 12:16

Sometimes we overeat and gain too much weight!

Describe your situation in detail in the space below. Explain why you may need to diet.

____

____

____

____

____

____

____

____

____

Discuss the situation with your parents or a friend. Write three possible solutions to this problem on the lines below.

1.______________________________

2.______________________________

3 ______________________________

Put a star (*) in front of the solution that would seem most successful in reducing weight according to your circumstances.

INSTEAD

". . . I am prudent . . . ." Isaiah 10:13

Sometimes when we have an urge to do something which we know we should not do, it is better to think of something very exciting and do that instead. Here are some things you might wish to try.

Some are exciting, but others help in a very special way. Still others are just plain zany and fun.

Fold a sheet of paper into fourths. Then cut and staple, making a booklet of eight pages. Write one aid to self-control on each page and illustrate it from your own experience. You might show some of the problems that would prompt you to do some of these things.

1. Read the funnies; see a funny show.
2. Watch a baby play; watch little animals play.
3. Let the wind blow your hair.
4. Wear sloppy, funny clothes.
5. Doodle!
6. Dance to some music—interpretative, aerobic, free!
7. Sing a song—make up the tune and words. Hit a real high note! Whistle!
8. Eat a meal with your wrong hand—right or left.
9. Throw a rock into the water, or splash in some water—a puddle or sprinkler.
10. Pick some flowers and weeds; smell them, hold them, crush them and smell the fresh green odor.
11. Wonder at the beauty of creation: flowers, birds, trees budding into leaf, clouds, snowflakes.
12. Pray—be still; let God look at you, and you look at God.
13. Make a list of things you would like to do alone.
14. Make a list of things you would like to do with your friends.
15. Think of something which nobody else would think of!

ROLE-PLAYING

"And to knowledge temperance; and to temperance patience; and to patience godliness."

II Peter 1:6

1. Decorate an old hatbox (or a box of another shape) and put a hole at the top.
2. Keep it supplied with small strips of paper that give situations where self-control is needed. Children may contribute these.
3. Divide the class into groups. Have each group select one slip of paper from the box.
4. Each group must role-play the situation explained on the paper.

HELPLESS?

". . . first be reconciled to thy brother, and then come and offer thy gift."
Matthew 5:24

Some people say we are living in an age of violence. We hear news of terrorists, gangs, and shootings and are encouraged to respond in the same manner. We forget the response that Jesus shows us in Matthew 5:21-26, 43-48, or what God tells through Moses in Exodus 20:13 and Deuteronomy 5:17. We also forget the advice Paul gives in I Corinthians 3:16,17. And often we think we are helpless to do anything about the world's situation. But are we?

Read these references found in your Bible. Then monitor the TV programs which you watch this week. In the space below, make a list of the incidents which show violence. Are the incidents shown as being wrong or as being all right?

Pick out one which shows violence as being all right. Rewrite the story to tell how it might have been written to avoid the violence, and yet make it an interesting story. Is the ending exciting?

Share your story with others and talk with them about it. You may wish to send or take this revised story to the manager of the TV station in your city and ask him to consider it.

SELF-CONTROL SEARCH

"That the aged men be sober, grave, temperate, sound in faith, in charity, in patience."

Titus 2:2

Listed below are some of the words we use in thinking when the Holy Spirit helps us control ourselves, as well as some that affect us adversely if we do not listen to Him.

See if you can find these words in the puzzle. Some letters are used more than once. The words may be found across, up, down, diagonally, or backward.

L	O	V	E	N	E	R	A	T	E	F
K	N	O	W	L	E	D	G	E	S	N
H	I	N	S	I	G	H	T	N	T	R
A	O	T	E	N	H	T	E	C	E	E
S	L	N	O	W	I	S	D	O	M	C
U	A	R	O	R	W	A	M	U	E	S
F	W	I	L	R	O	F	P	R	R	I
F	U	N	D	E	R	S	T	A	N	D
E	F	T	R	V	K	E	H	G	T	O
R	A	E	F	E	E	P	I	E	T	Y
E	I	G	J	R	E	N	V	S	L	S
S	T	R	A	E	B	A	D	O	R	E
P	H	I	U	S	R	B	H	U	I	I
E	L	T	B	B	E	T	T	E	R	L
C	E	Y	A	R	P	J	U	D	G	E
T	E	V	O	C	E	U	T	R	I	V

WORDS:

adore
covet
honor
knowledge
pray
understand
work

bear
discern
holy
law
piety
endure
wrong

brave
faith
integrity
lies
revere
venerate

better
fear
insight
love
respect
virtue

courage
fast
judge
pain
suffer
wisdom

HIPPITY-HOP

"For where your treasure is, there will your heart be also."
Matthew 6:21

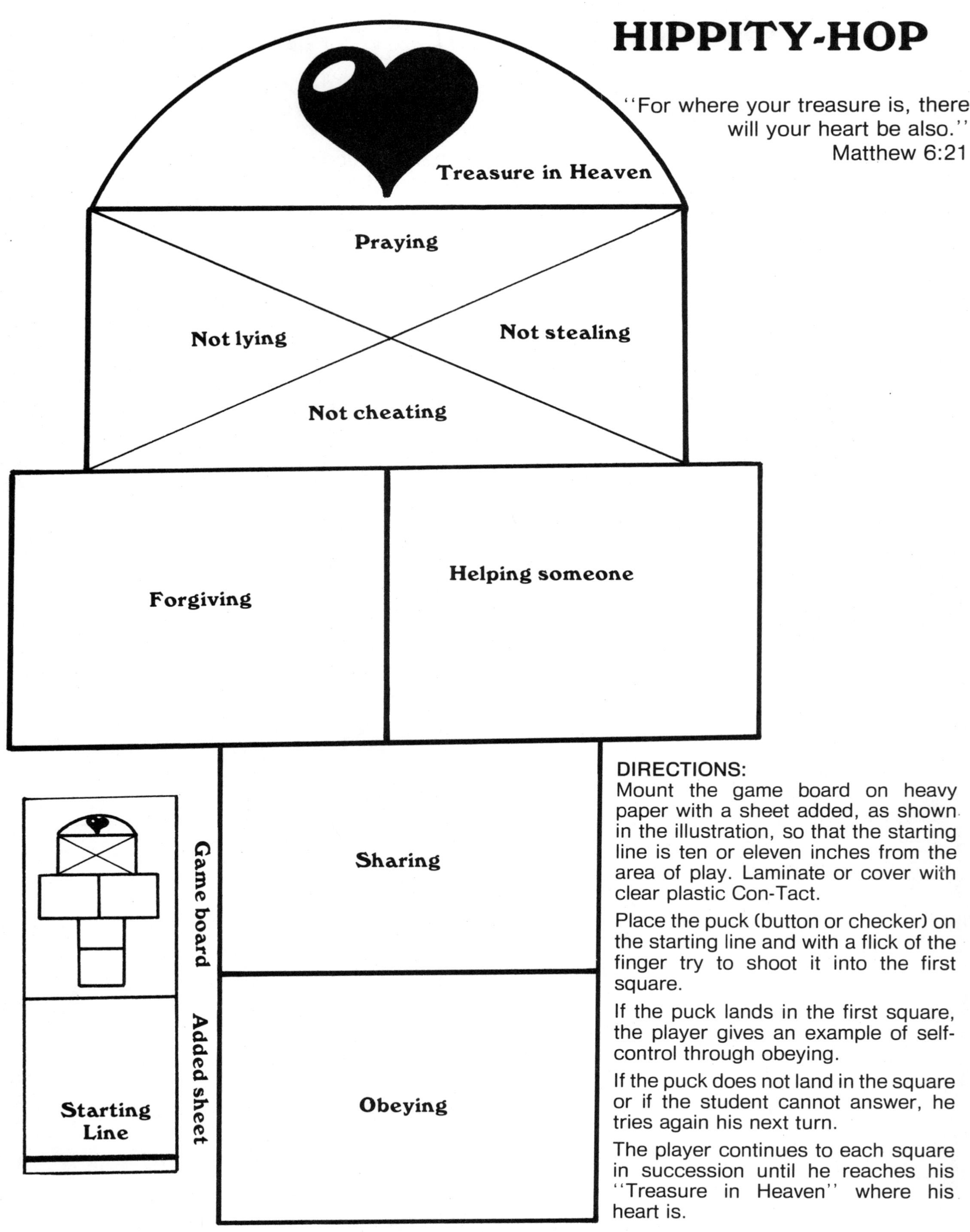

DIRECTIONS:
Mount the game board on heavy paper with a sheet added, as shown in the illustration, so that the starting line is ten or eleven inches from the area of play. Laminate or cover with clear plastic Con-Tact.

Place the puck (button or checker) on the starting line and with a flick of the finger try to shoot it into the first square.

If the puck lands in the first square, the player gives an example of self-control through obeying.

If the puck does not land in the square or if the student cannot answer, he tries again his next turn.

The player continues to each square in succession until he reaches his "Treasure in Heaven" where his heart is.

DECISIONS! DECISIONS!

"A prudent man foreseeth the evil . . . ." Proverbs 22:3

The gift of courage helps us control our natural reactions to events, so that we may keep from doing something wrong or hurtful. Tell how these children might have reacted in the following situations, and explain your answers.

1. Jeanne's mother called her to get up. Jeanne knew she should, but she was so snug and warm she hated to get out of bed. If she didn't get up right away, she would miss her morning prayers, and there were many things about the day she should talk over with God. What might some of these things be? How could self-control help her?

____

____

____

____

____

2. Jack went out to play at recess with the other boys. He wanted to play keep away, but the other boys wanted to play kick ball. They made fun of Jack when they saw he was disappointed. This made Jack angry. How would self-control have helped Jack to choose what was right? How would it have helped the other boys?

____

____

____

____

____

3. Karen wouldn't talk to Jan because Jan went skating with another friend and didn't invite Karen. How could self-control help Karen in her reaction to Jan? How could it have helped Jan?

____

____

____

____

____

ONE TO GROW ON

"Know ye not that they which run in a race run all, but one receiveth the prize? So run, that ye may obtain." I Corinthians 9:24

We grow in self-control by practicing over and over. Paul tells us in I Corinthians 9:24-27 that we must strive as an athlete does. A swimmer or an olympic gymnast practices many hours a day to become a gold medalist. We, too, must do hard things again and again to grow in character. Practice helps us develop habits that will become part of us.

Here is a list of things to practice. Pick one. Do it once a week, for instance every Sunday or every Tuesday, or once a day. Soon you will find that it will not be so hard any more. Focus on just one project so you do not tire of trying too many.

Make a poster to hang in your room to remind you to discipline yourself.

1. Give up a favorite food—ice cream, candy—once a week.
2. Give money, saved by abstaining from snacks, to a missionary or to the poor in your city.
3. Refrain from watching TV once a week. Plan a family time instead.
4. Attend church every Sunday.
5. Pray quietly every morning to thank God for the promise of another day.
6. Try one of the "shoulds" you never get around to doing. For example, "I should pick up my clothes before going to school."
7. Visit a nursing home. Take a surprise.
8. Write a letter to someone who is lonely. Pick a certain day to do this.
9. Write a letter to your grandmother or grandfather every other Tuesday.
10. Do something you find hard to remember:
    a. Put your shoes at the foot of your bed each evening where you can find them the next morning.
    b. Brush your teeth carefully each morning and evening.
    c. Polish your shoes every Saturday.
11. Just before you go to sleep say a special prayer for someone who needs it.
12. Choose something which you know you need to work on in your life.

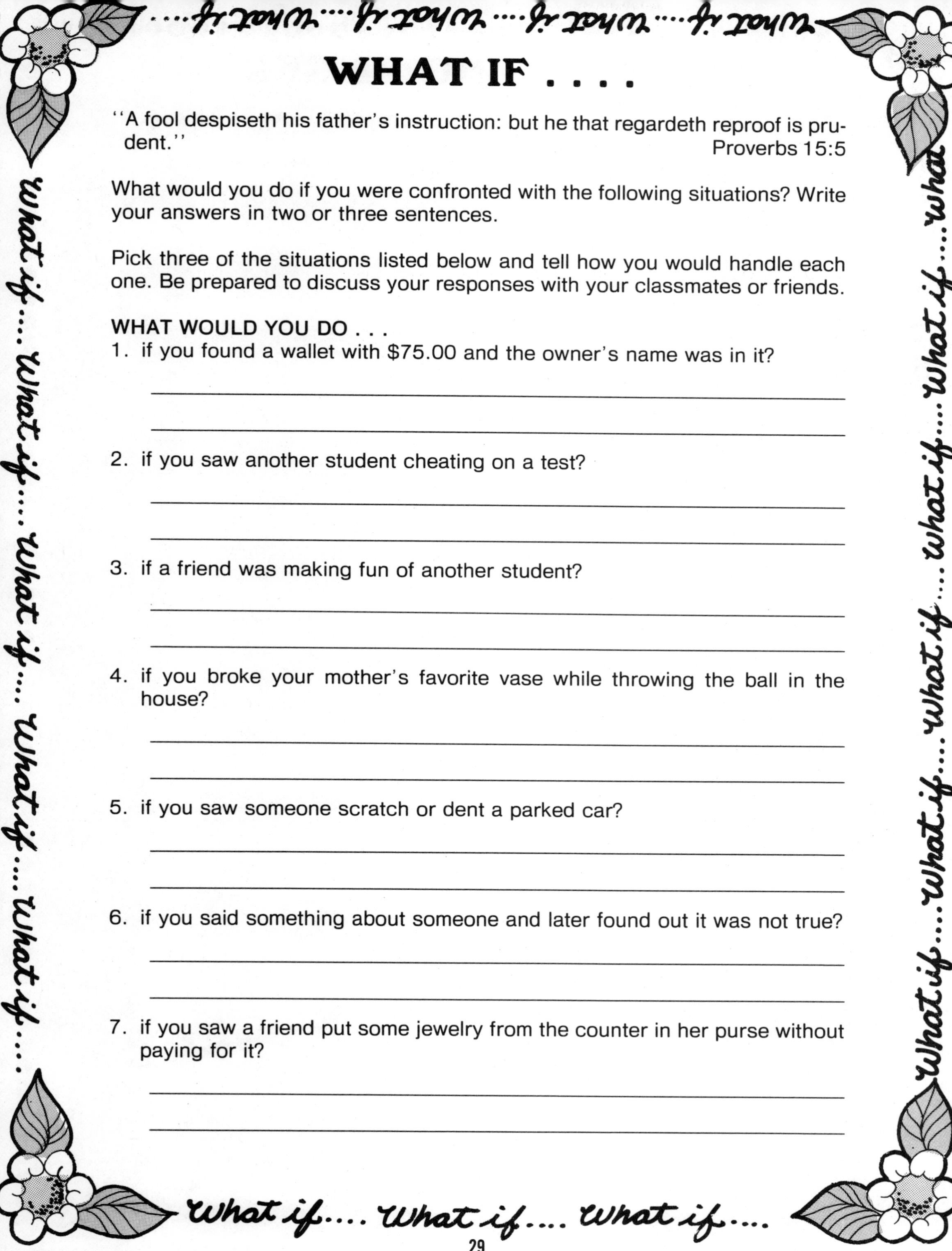

WHAT IF . . . .

"A fool despiseth his father's instruction: but he that regardeth reproof is prudent."
Proverbs 15:5

What would you do if you were confronted with the following situations? Write your answers in two or three sentences.

Pick three of the situations listed below and tell how you would handle each one. Be prepared to discuss your responses with your classmates or friends.

WHAT WOULD YOU DO . . .

1. if you found a wallet with $75.00 and the owner's name was in it?

   ____

   ____

2. if you saw another student cheating on a test?

   ____

   ____

3. if a friend was making fun of another student?

   ____

   ____

4. if you broke your mother's favorite vase while throwing the ball in the house?

   ____

   ____

5. if you saw someone scratch or dent a parked car?

   ____

   ____

6. if you said something about someone and later found out it was not true?

   ____

   ____

7. if you saw a friend put some jewelry from the counter in her purse without paying for it?

   ____

   ____

EXPRESSING ANGER

"Therefore the prudent shall keep silence in that time . . . ." Amos 5:13

Anger is a feeling we all have at times. It should be expressed in appropriate ways.

A. Give a recent example of a person, situation or thing that caused you to be angry.

____

____

____

B. List some healthy ways to express anger.

____

____

____

C. List some unhealthy ways to express anger.

____

____

____

D. Explain how you caused someone else to be angry.

____

____

____

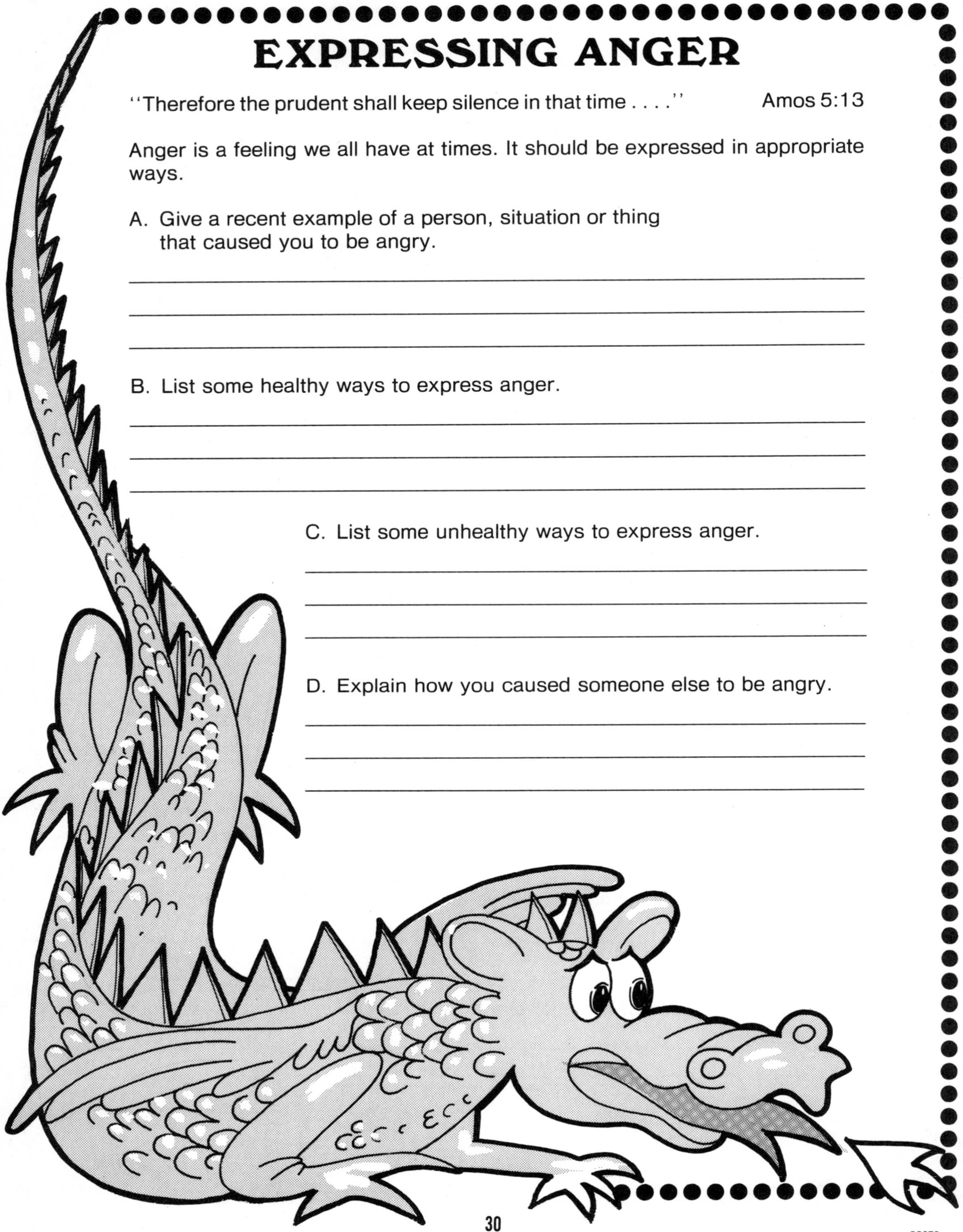

MAKE YOUR OWN TEMPERATURE GAUGE

"A soft answer turneth away wrath; but grievous words stir up anger."
Proverbs 15:1

Copy the pattern onto lightweight cardboard. Cut slits at the top and bottom of the thermometer. Use a red ribbon attached to a white ribbon to simulate the mercury. Attach in a circle through the slits around the thermometer. A temperature is indicated by putting the end of the red ribbon by the word that best describes how you would feel.

After you complete your temperature gauge, think about each situation listed below, and register how you would feel by moving the red ribbon up or down.

Your teacher criticized you in front of the whole class.

Your best friends went to the park and didn't invite you.

You studied for a test but didn't get a good mark.

Your mother forgot to do something that she promised she would do.

Your father said you should act more grown-up.

You must stay home from a party because you have to watch the baby while your mother shops.

Your team lost the championship game.

You can't find your pen.

BRAINSTORM for situations that can happen to you at home, in school, in play groups, etc., in which you would have a mild to strong emotional response.

Ask you friends to register their emotions on the thermometer too. Then discuss POSITIVE WAYS to handle each situation so your temperature will "cool down."

FURIOUS

ANGRY

FRUSTRATED

UPSET

EMBARRASSED

SURPRISED

HELPING OUR ENVIRONMENT

"You shall not defile the land in which you live . . . ." (RSV) Numbers 35:34

In 1854 an assembly was held in western Washington, during which Indians and government representatives signed land treaties.

Chief Seattle said:

> "The earth is precious to God, and to harm the earth is to heap contempt on its Creator."

Everyone must work to keep the environment healthy and pleasant. Here are some ways you and your family and friends can help:

1. Put all litter in a trash can. If you see litter on the ground, pick it up.
2. Cut down on noise pollution by playing stereos, radios, and televisions softly.
3. Save items that can be used again. We call this recycling.

Can you think of others? List them below:

4. ______________________________

5. ______________________________

6. ______________________________

7. ______________________________

8. ______________________________

TAKING ACTION

". . . the prudent are crowned with knowledge." Proverbs 14:18

Think of a way to improve a local litter problem. State the problem and explain your contribution to its solution. Send your idea to the health department in your city, and ask them to consider it.

ECOLOGY POSTER

Design a poster to convince others of the value of caring for the earth. Place it in a location where it will receive lots of attention.

CELEBRATING SELF-CONTROL

PATH TO SELF-CONTROL

DIRECTIONS:
To review what you have learned about self-control, work through the maze. Begin in the space marked START. Do each task in the order it appears on the path. Color each space as you finish the task. Continue working your way along the path until you reach the space marked FINISHED.

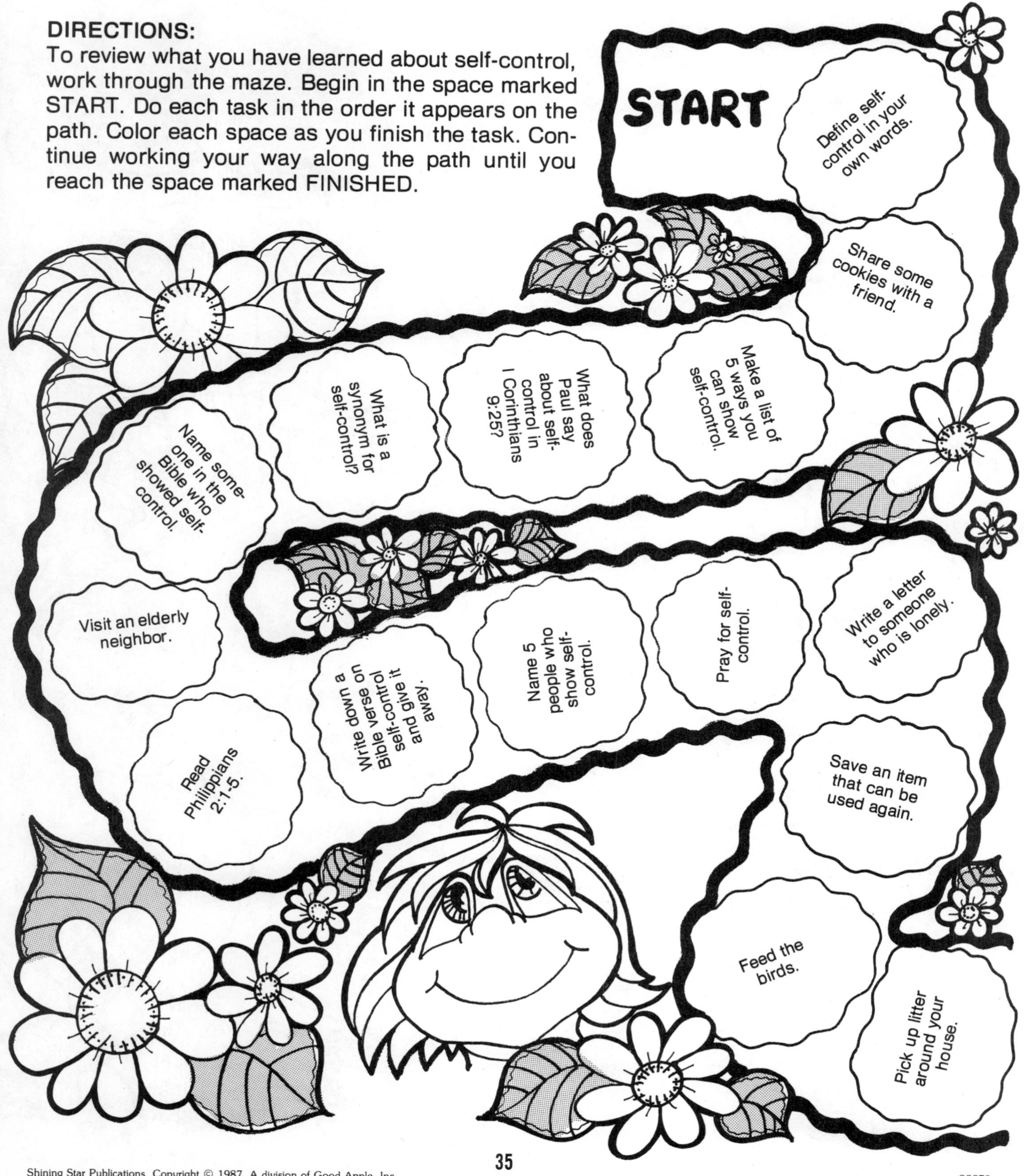

FINISH
Listen to your teacher.
Help your mom at home after school.
Give money to the poor.
Write a slogan about self-control.
List 3 ways your class can show self-control.
Ask your dad what self-control means to him.
Include a shy classmate in your game.
Obey your parents.
Read a story to your younger sister.
Clean your bedroom.
Let your brother watch his favorite TV show.
Using sign language, learn the sign for self-control.
Find a story of self-control in the Bible.
Give up a favorite food today.

FINGER PUPPETS

". . . the fruit of the Spirit is . . . temperance . . . ." Galatians 5:22,23

Make a finger puppet for each of your fingers. Let each finger puppet represent someone who has caused you to be angry and tested your self-control. Share with a friend the different situations involved with each one.

FOR EXAMPLE:
Todd borrows your pencil and breaks it . . . Dana talks about you to her friends . . . Mark pushes you in line . . . Michele talks in class and blames it on you . . . Raymond trips you and then laughs . . . .

HERE ARE SOME PATTERNS FOR YOU:

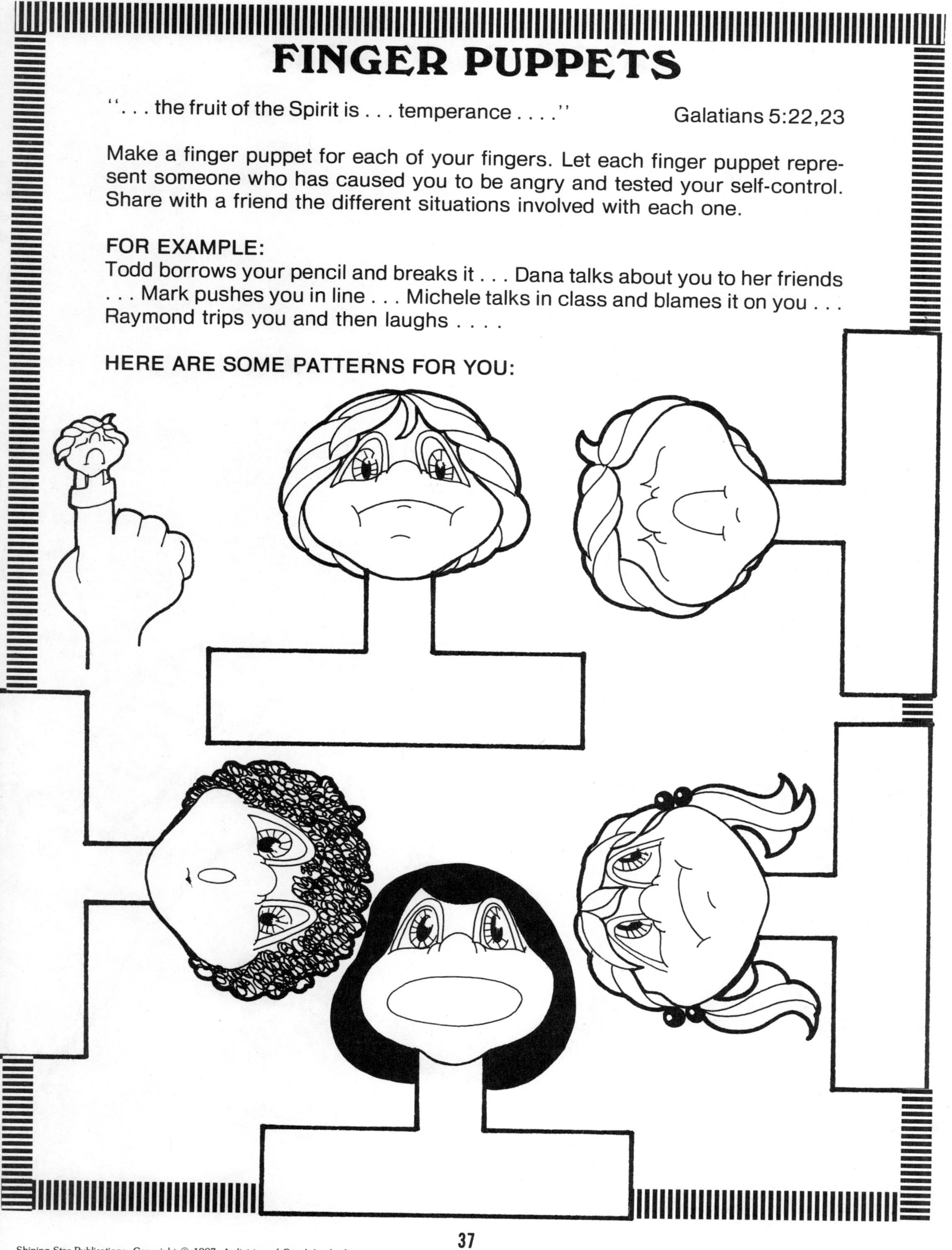

PEANUT BLOSSOMS

"... the prudent are crowned with knowlege." Proverbs 14:18

INGREDIENTS:

1 ¾ cup flour
1 tsp. baking soda
¼ tsp. salt
½ cup sugar
½ cup firmly packed brown sugar
½ cup shortening
½ cup peanut butter
1 egg
2 tbsp. milk
1 tsp. vanilla
48 chocolate kisses

DIRECTIONS:

1. Combine all ingredients except candy in large mixing bowl.
2. Mix on lowest speed until dough forms.
3. Shape dough into balls using a rounded teaspoon for each.
4. Roll balls in sugar and place on ungreased cookie sheets.
5. Bake at 375° for 10-12 minutes.
6. Cool 2 minutes on sheet.
7. Top each cookie with a chocolate kiss. Press down firmly so cookie comes up around edge of candy.
8. Practice SELF-CONTROL and share cookies with your friends!

SOUP-ER KIDS WITH SELF-CONTROL

"And every man that striveth for the mastery is temperate in all things . . . ."
I Corinthians 9:25

OBJECTIVE: This bulletin board shows the names of those students who have exhibited self-control during the week.

PROCEDURE:
1. Draw a large pot and print the words "Soup-er Kids with Self-Control" on it.
2. Insert spoons with the names of those children who have shown this virtue. Tongue depressors make good spoons, or use spoon pattern found on page 40.

VARIATIONS: Other appropriate titles could be
"Stir Up Some Self-control"
"Soup-er Passages on Self-Control"

POT PATTERN

MAKE A MOVIE

"Behold, my servant shall deal prudently, he shall be exalted and extolled, and be very high."
Isaiah 52:13

1. Ask each student to prepare a story demonstrating a situation of self-control, which may be made into a movie.
2. Give each student a length of adding machine tape at least one yard long.
3. Have each student divide the tape into several frames. Each frame should contain a line from the story and a colorful illustration.
4. Explain and demonstrate to the class how individual frames are combined to make a filmstrip.
5. Construct a "theater" for your filmstrip using a shoe box and two pencils, as illustrated.

PROJECT POTPOURRI

"I wisdom dwell with prudence, and find out knowledge of witty inventions."
Proverbs 8:12

FEED THE BIRDS

Some birds change their homes as the seasons change, but many do not. They live in the northern areas all the time and in warm seasons go even farther north. Birds that remain in areas where the ground is covered with ice and snow sometimes have a hard time finding food. How can humans help them?

Put suet in a mesh bag and tie the top securely. Hang it from a tree limb. Or place the suet in a soap dish. Tie the soap dish to the trunk of a tree. Observe from a distance what kinds of birds come to eat.

SIGN LANGUAGE

Learn the sign for "self-control."

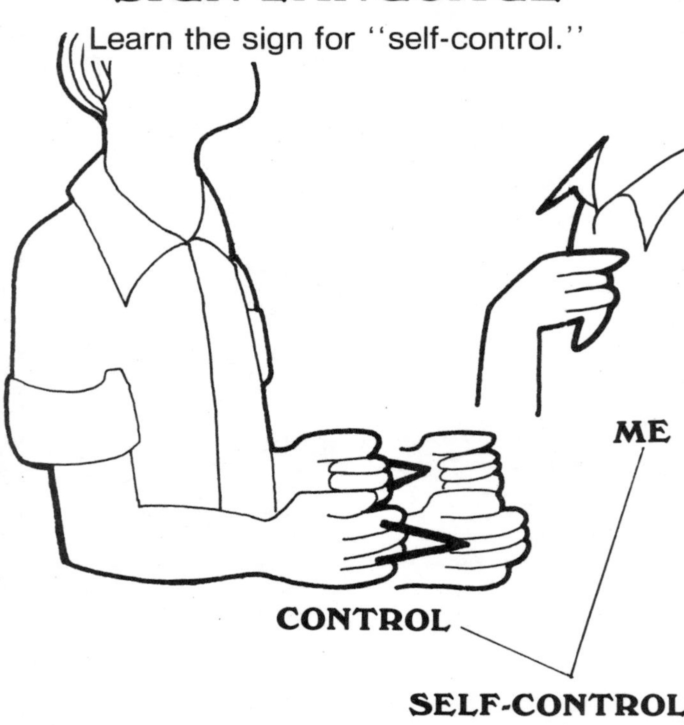

MAKE A GIFT

String beads and make a necklace or bracelet for your mom! Take your time.

BUILD A TERRARIUM

". . . a time to build . . . ." Ecclesiastes 3:3

Build your own woodland terrarium. Mosses, small ferns, lichens, liverworts, and tiny Virginia creepers make interesting plants for this project. A live, small toad or live salamander may be added. Research what foods they will need in order to survive.

To add to the enjoyment of your classroom terrarium, keep a good magnifying glass close by. Your students will be able to see so much more happening.

Never use soap or any detergent to clean the container for a terrarium. Use water and a handful of coarse salt to rub soiled spots.

SELF-CONTROL EXPERT
to ____________

YOU'RE SUPER

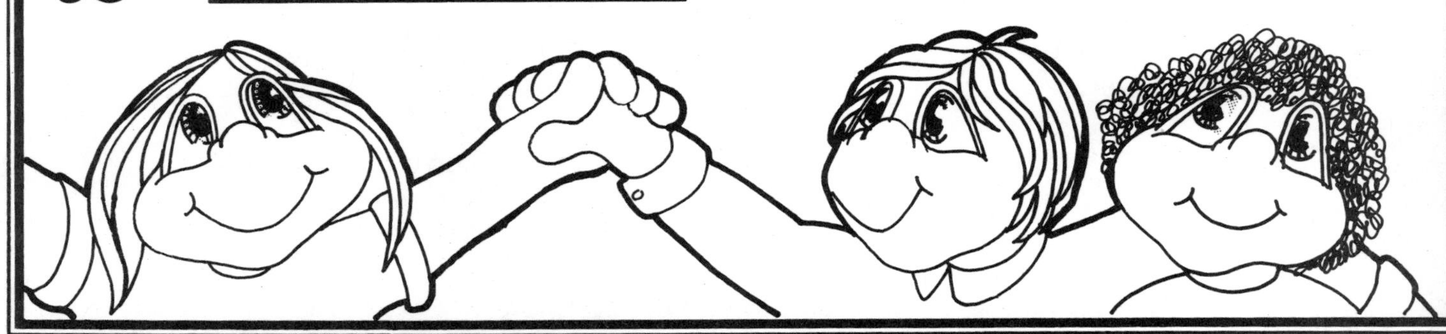

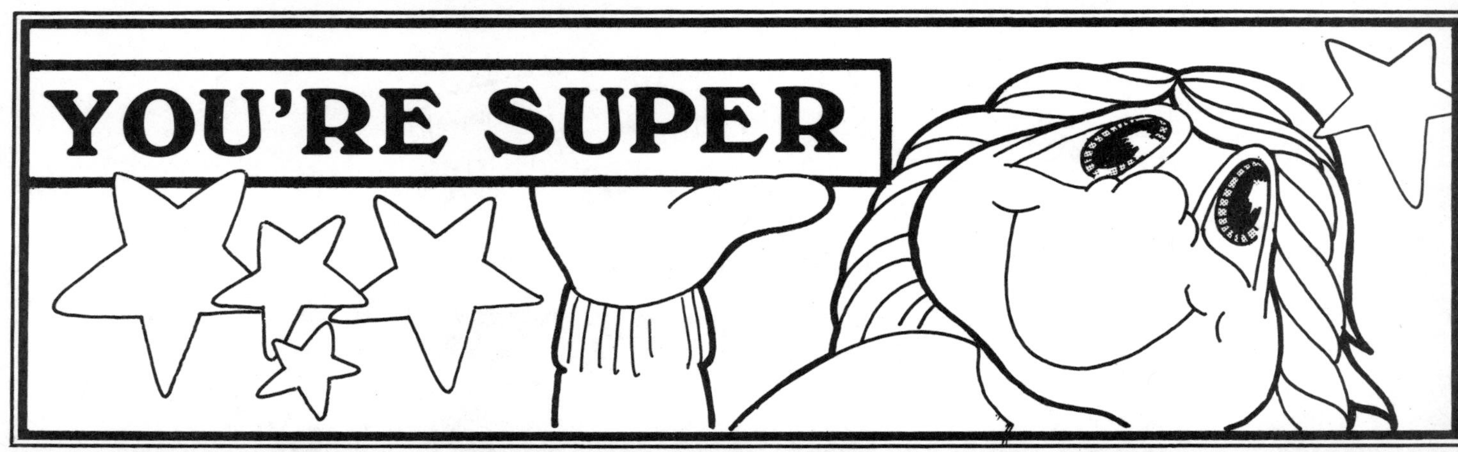

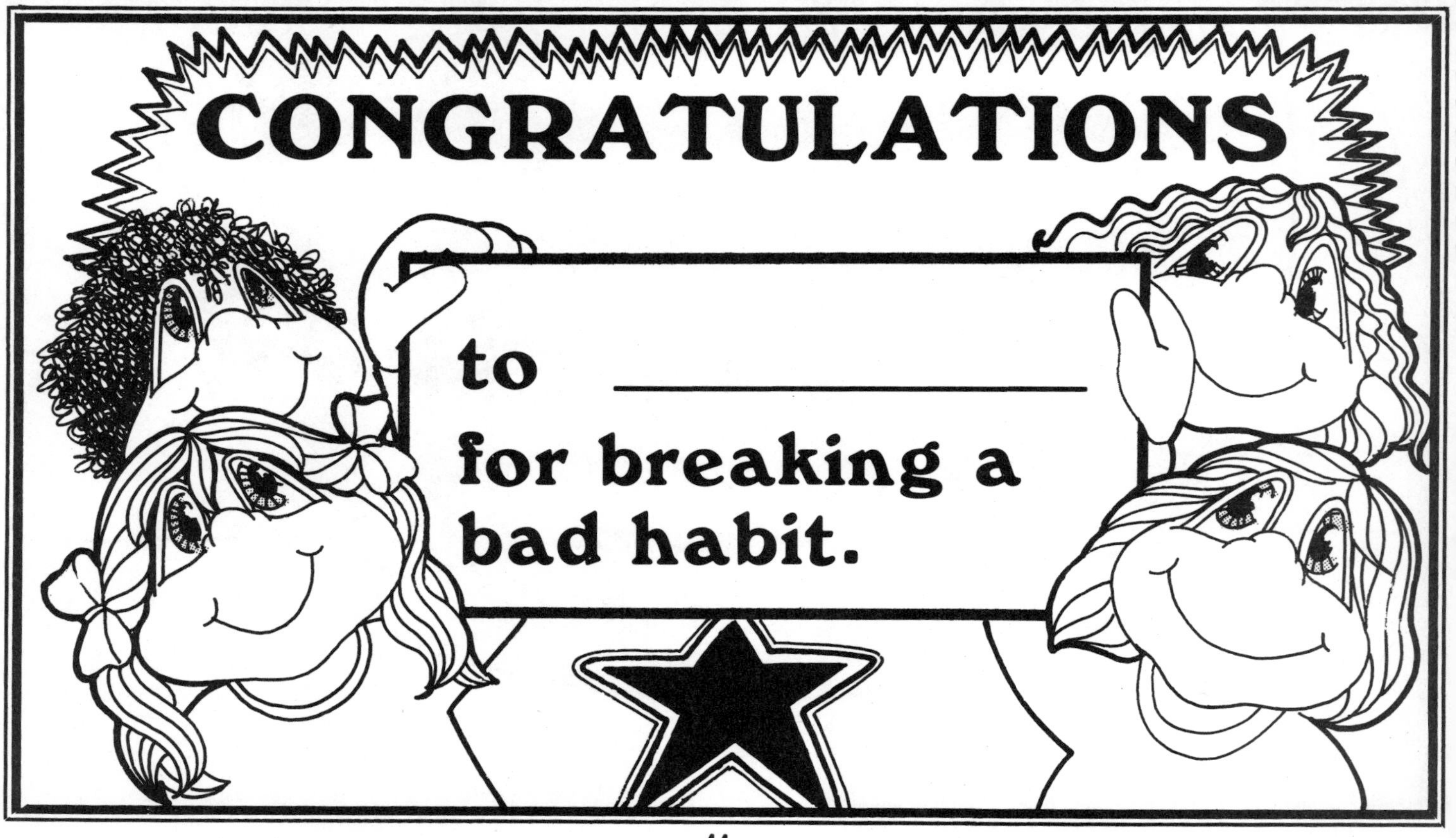
CONGRATULATIONS
to ____________
for breaking a bad habit.

PRAYER CELEBRATION OF SELF-CONTROL

Before the prayer celebration, gather the children and seat them in groups on blankets outside on the lawn.

OPENING HYMN: ''Sing Unto the Lord,'' p.46

PRAYER: God, our Father, even though we like to have our own things, we must learn self-control and share what we have with others. Help us always find happiness in giving of ourselves.

FIRST READING: Paul's letter to the Philippians, 2:1-5 (an adaptation)
Do not do things only for yourself. Always think of other people. Have happiness and joy in knowing that you are working with others and sharing with them.

SECOND READING: Matthew 14:13-21 (an adaptation)
Jesus went by boat to a deserted place. Many people found out he was going and followed Him on land. When Jesus arrived and got out of the boat, many people were there to greet Him. He took pity on them and healed them and preached to them for a very long time.
Evening came and Jesus realized the people had nothing to eat. A little boy gave Jesus his lunch to share with the others. Jesus took the five loaves of bread and two fishes. After he gave thanks to His Father, He broke the bread into pieces and gave them to His Disciples to distribute to the crowd.
(At this time baskets of breadsticks, crackers or rolls are given to each group of children. While instrumental music is playing, they eat their treat. When the children have finished, the reader asks for silence . . . .)

The Disciples collected twelve baskets of fragments that were left over.

(Representatives from each group collect the baskets of left-overs.)

BLESSING: Let us go forth and always share what we have with others!

CLOSING HYMN: ''Fruit of the Spirit,'' page 46.

FRUIT OF THE SPIRIT
Music by Helen Friesen
Words from Gal. 5:22-23
F Bb C7 F C F
The fruit of the Spir-it is love, joy, peace, long suf-fer-ing gen-tle-
F Bb F C7 F Gm F C7 F
ness, good-ness, faith, Meek-ness, self-control: a-gainst such there is no law.
SING UNTO THE LORD
Music by Helen Friesen
Words from Ps. 96:2
Sing un-to the Lord, bless his name; shew forth his sal-va-tion from day to
day. Sing un-to the Lord, bless his name; shew forth his sal-va-tion.
from day to day

ANSWER KEY

FOLLOWING JESUS p. 7

1. 3 H
2. 2 E/F
3. 2/3 C/D
4. 5/6 B/C
5. 3 H
6. 2/3 C/D
7. 5 D/E
8. 2/3 C
9. 3 H
10. 2/3 F
11. 5 D/E
12. 2/3 C
13. 2/3 C/D
14. 2/3 F
15. 2 E/F
16. 3 H
17. 3 H
18. 4 B
19. 2 E/F
20. 3 H

SEVEN YEARS OF FAMINE p. 13

1. coat of many colors
2. The stars, sun and moon bowed down before him.
3. to take food to them
4. Joseph
5. He would get his job back.
6. He would be hanged in three days.
7. seven good ears of corn and seven dried ears of corn or seven fat cows and seven lean cows
8. seven good years followed by seven years of famine
9. Egypt
10. to store food for the famine
11. by storing food for the famine
12. to get food
13. Benjamin
14. He was their brother.
15. This was part of God's plan.

PAUL'S MESSAGE p. 14

We exult in sufferings also knowing that suffering works endurance and endurance produces virtue, and virtue hope. And hope does not disappoint, because the love of God is poured forth in our hearts by the Holy Spirit who has been given to us.

SELF-CONTROL SEARCH p. 25

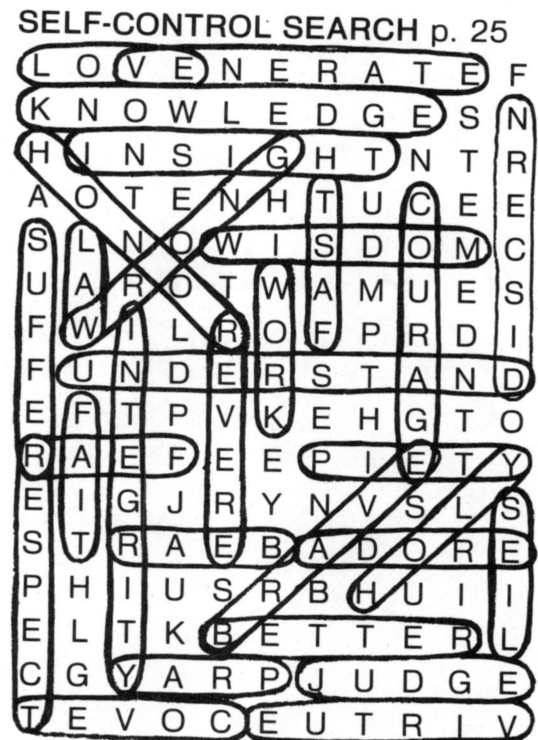

SCRIPTURAL PASSAGES ON SELF-CONTROL

I Samuel 16:18
II Chronicles 2:12
Proverbs 8:12; 8:15; 12:16; 12:23; 13:16; 14:8; 14:15; 14:18; 15:5; 19:14; 22:3; 27:12
Isaiah 3:2; 5:21; 10:13; 52:13
Jeremiah 49:7
Hosea 14:9
Amos 5:13
Matthew 11:25
Luke 10:21
Acts 13:7; 24:25
I Corinthians 1:19; 9:25
Galatians 5:23
Ephesians 1:8
Titus 1:7; 1:8; 2:2
II Peter 1:6; 2:10